Cross Stitch

Seasonal Cottages

Adorn your home with cute cottages all year!

Designs by Alma Lynne Hayden

2

16

24

LEISURE ARTS, INC. • Maumelle, Arkansas

Spring Cottage

Celebrate the splendors of spring with this delightful bungalow.

Note: Please read all instructions on page 32 before beginning.

Stitch Count = 125w × 125h

FABRIC SIZE

- One 17" × 17" (43.2cm × 43.2cm) piece of 28-ct. Summer Sky Hand-Dyed Jobelan® by Wichelt Imports (stitched over two threads)

DESIGN SIZE

- 25-ct. = 10" × 10" (25.4cm × 25.4cm)
- 28-ct. = $8\frac{7}{8}$" × $8\frac{7}{8}$" (22.5cm × 22.5cm)
- 32-ct. = $7\frac{7}{8}$" × $7\frac{7}{8}$" (20.0cm × 20.0cm)

Project Tip

Prevent Twisting

During the movement of stitching, the needle naturally twists, which can cause loops and knots in the thread. To prevent this, work several stitches, then make note of which way the thread unwinds when you hang it straight down from your work. Give your needle a partial turn in that direction with each stitch to keep the thread from twisting.

SPRING COTTAGE CHART DIAGRAM

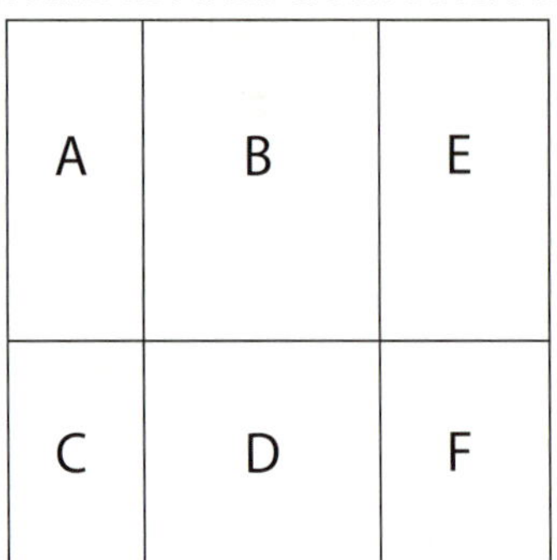

Spring Cottage A

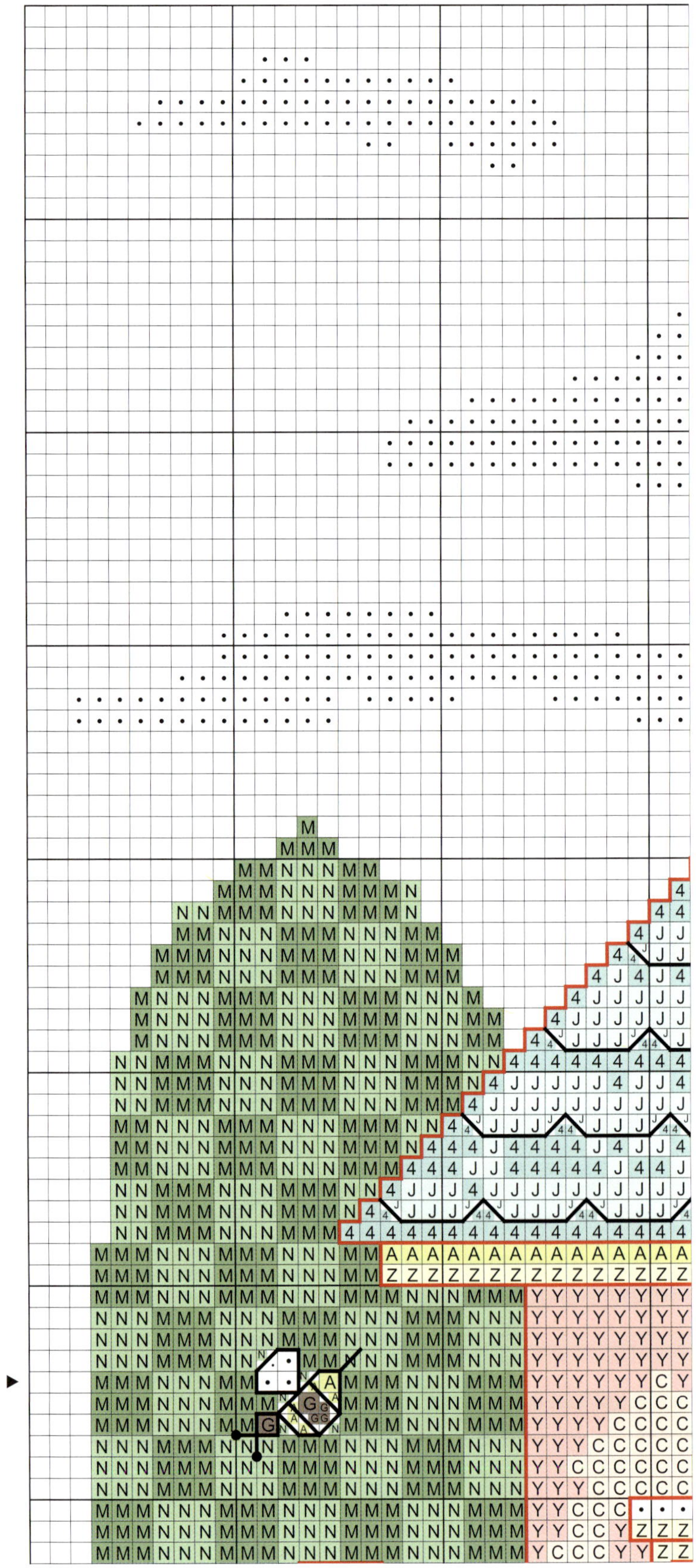

CROSS STITCH

ANCHOR		DMC	COLOR
002	•	White	White
109	V	209	Dark Lavender
9046	S	321	Christmas Red
977	H	334	Medium Baby Blue
273	E	535	Very Light Ash Gray
302	A	743	Medium Yellow
301	Z	744	Pale Yellow
1021	Y	761	Light Salmon
257	M	905	Dark Parrot Green
256	N	906	Medium Parrot Green
255	7	907	Light Parrot Green
186	4	959	Medium Sea Green
076	F	961	Dark Dusty Rose
185	J	964	Light Sea Green
355	P	975	Dark Golden Brown
1001	L	976	Medium Golden Brown
382	G	3371	Black Brown
1020	C	3713	Very Light Salmon
140	K	3755	Baby Blue
188	D	3812	Very Dark Sea Green
311	2	3827	Pale Golden Brown

FRENCH KNOT

ANCHOR		DMC	COLOR
382	•	3371	Black Brown

BACKSTITCH

ANCHOR		DMC	COLOR
273	—	535	Very Light Ash Gray
257	—	905	Dark Parrot Green
355	—	975	Dark Golden Brown
382	—	3371	Black Brown

Gray area indicates last row of previous section of design.

CROSS STITCH

ANCHOR		DMC	COLOR
002	•	White	White
109	V	209	Dark Lavender
9046	S	321	Christmas Red
977	H	334	Medium Baby Blue
273	E	535	Very Light Ash Gray
302	A	743	Medium Yellow
301	Z	744	Pale Yellow
1021	Y	761	Light Salmon
257	M	905	Dark Parrot Green
256	N	906	Medium Parrot Green
255	7	907	Light Parrot Green
186	4	959	Medium Sea Green
076	F	961	Dark Dusty Rose
185	J	964	Light Sea Green
355	P	975	Dark Golden Brown
1001	L	976	Medium Golden Brown
382	G	3371	Black Brown
1020	C	3713	Very Light Salmon
140	K	3755	Baby Blue
188	D	3812	Very Dark Sea Green
311	2	3827	Pale Golden Brown

FRENCH KNOT

ANCHOR		DMC	COLOR
382	•	3371	Black Brown

BACKSTITCH

ANCHOR		DMC	COLOR
273	—	535	Very Light Ash Gray
257	—	905	Dark Parrot Green
355	—	975	Dark Golden Brown
382	—	3371	Black Brown

Gray area indicates last row of previous section of design.

Spring Cottage C

Spring Cottage D

CROSS STITCH

ANCHOR		DMC	COLOR
002	•	White	White
109	V	209	Dark Lavender
9046	S	321	Christmas Red
977	H	334	Medium Baby Blue
273	E	535	Very Light Ash Gray
302	A	743	Medium Yellow
301	Z	744	Pale Yellow
1021	Y	761	Light Salmon
257	M	905	Dark Parrot Green
256	N	906	Medium Parrot Green
255	7	907	Light Parrot Green
186	4	959	Medium Sea Green
076	F	961	Dark Dusty Rose
185	J	964	Light Sea Green
355	P	975	Dark Golden Brown
1001	L	976	Medium Golden Brown
382	G	3371	Black Brown
1020	C	3713	Very Light Salmon
140	K	3755	Baby Blue
188	D	3812	Very Dark Sea Green
311	2	3827	Pale Golden Brown

FRENCH KNOT

ANCHOR		DMC	COLOR
382	•	3371	Black Brown

BACKSTITCH

ANCHOR		DMC	COLOR
273	(blue line)	535	Very Light Ash Gray
257	(green line)	905	Dark Parrot Green
355	(red line)	975	Dark Golden Brown
382	(black line)	3371	Black Brown

Gray area indicates last row of previous section of design.

Spring Cottage E

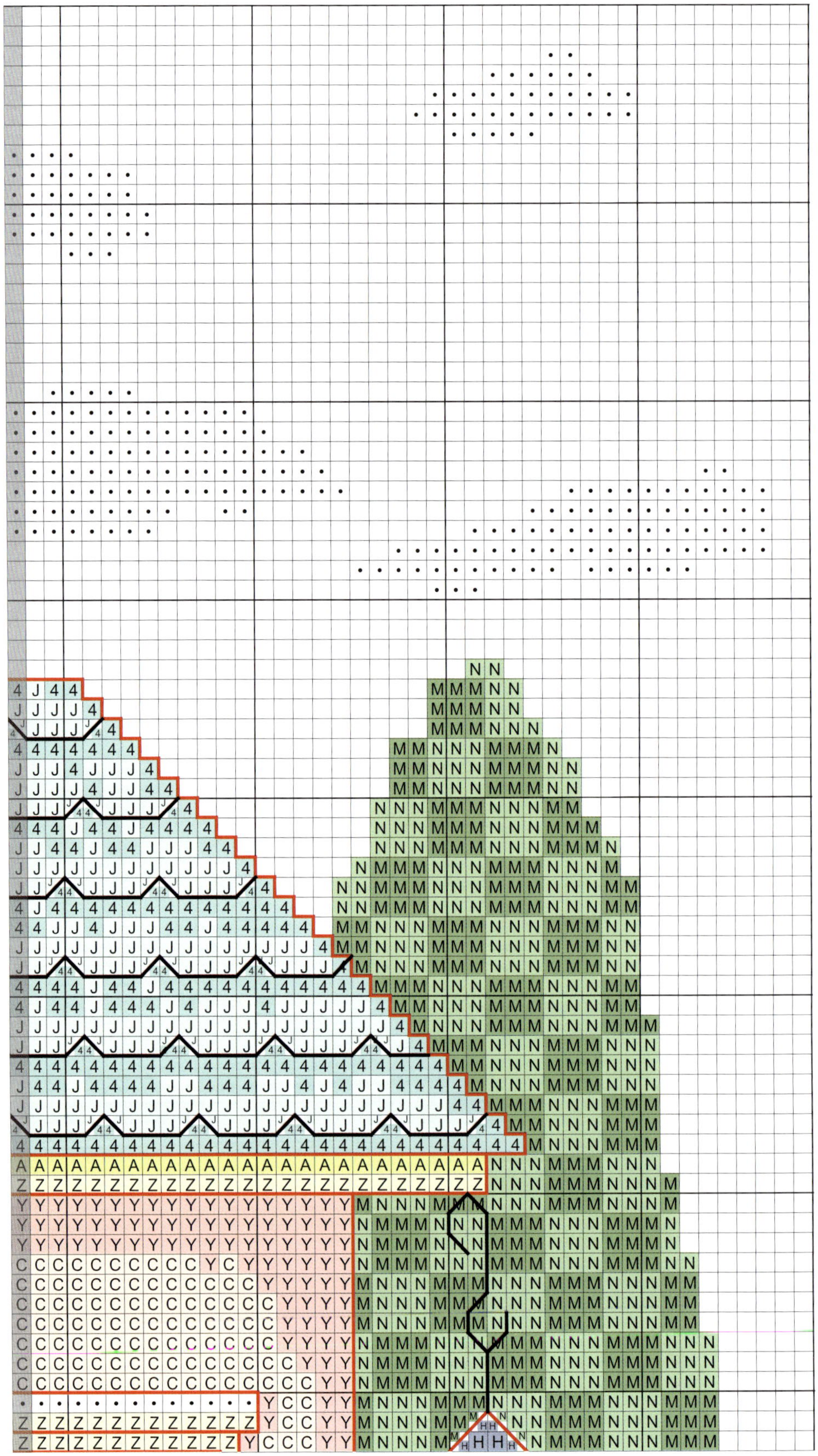

Spring Cottage F

Summer Cottage

Enjoy a lazy summer day

with this charming beachside retreat.

Note: Please read all instructions on page 32 before beginning.

Stitch Count = 125w × 124h

FABRIC SIZE

- One 17" × 17" (43.2cm × 43.2cm) piece of 28-ct. Summer Sky Hand-Dyed Jobelan® by Wichelt Imports (stitched over two threads)

DESIGN SIZE

- 25-ct. = 10" × 10" (25.4cm × 25.4cm)
- 28-ct. = 8⁷/₈" × 8⁷/₈" (22.5cm × 22.5cm)
- 32-ct. = 7⁷/₈" × 7⁷/₈" (20.0cm × 20.0cm)

SUMMER COTTAGE CHART DIAGRAM

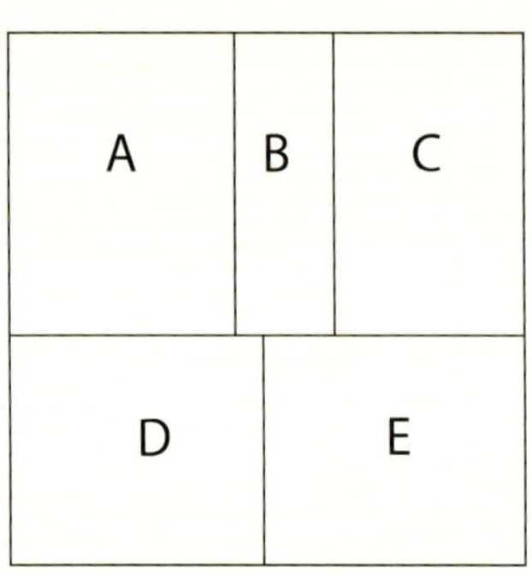

CROSS STITCH

ANCHOR		DMC	COLOR
002	•	White	White
109	V	209	Dark Lavender
9046	S	321	Christmas Red
977	H	334	Medium Baby Blue
302	A	743	Medium Yellow
301	Z	744	Pale Yellow
300	M	745	Light Pale Yellow
234	Q	762	Very Light Pearl Gray
128	F	775	Very Light Baby Blue
132	E	797	Royal Blue
256	N	906	Medium Parrot Green
255	7	907	Light Parrot Green
040	C	956	Geranium
050	B	957	Pale Geranium
186	I	959	Medium Sea Green
185	J	964	Light Sea Green
355	P	975	Dark Golden Brown
129	G	3325	Light Baby Blue
899	O	3782	Light Mocha Brown

FRENCH KNOT

ANCHOR		DMC	COLOR
002	•	White	White
132	•	797	Royal Blue

BACKSTITCH

ANCHOR		DMC	COLOR
132	—	797	Royal Blue
256	—	906	Medium Parrot Green
355	—	975	Dark Golden Brown

STRAIGHT STITCH

ANCHOR		DMC	COLOR
132	—	797	Royal Blue
355	—	975	Dark Golden Brown

Gray area indicates last row of previous section of design.

Summer Cottage A

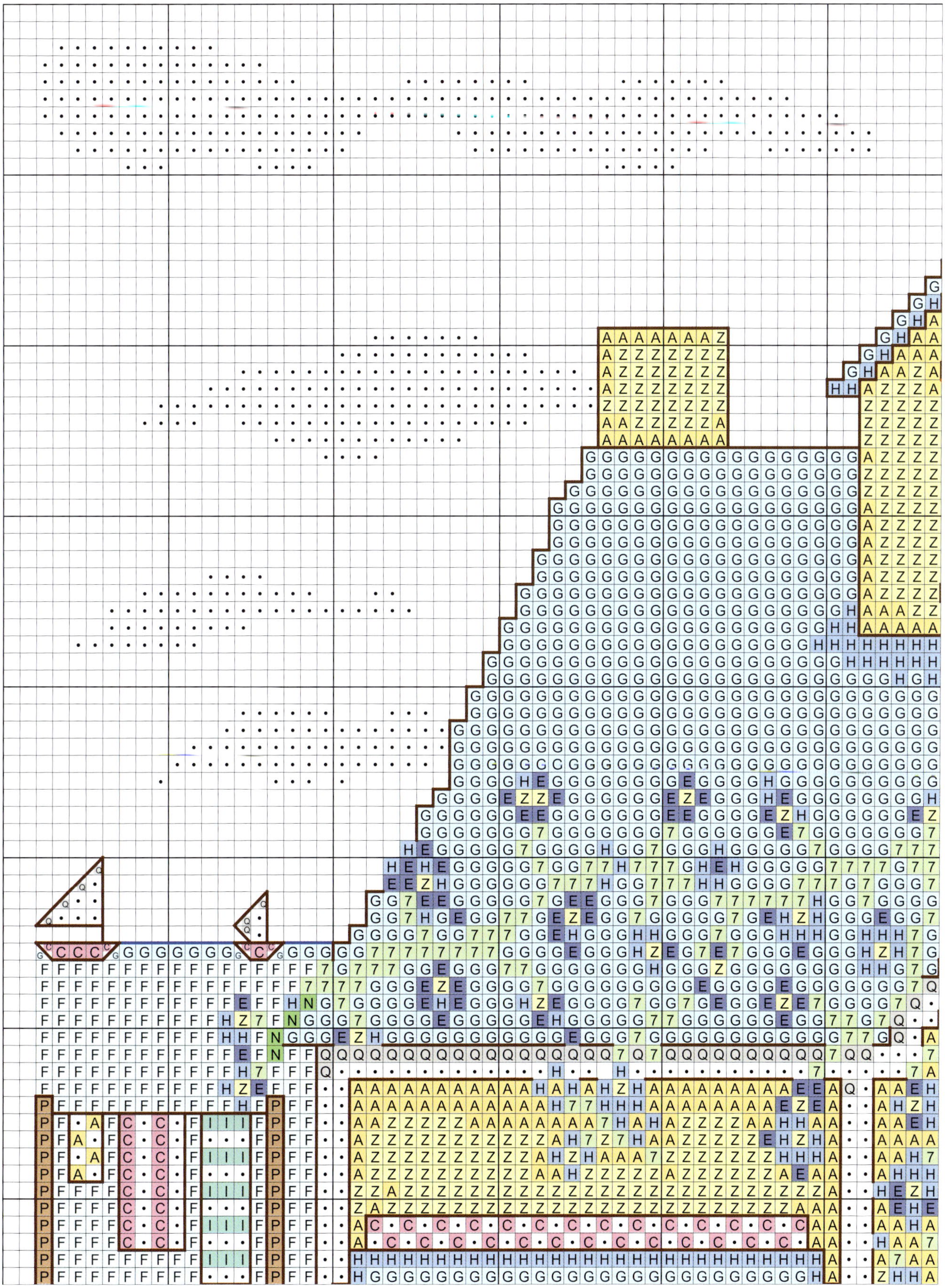

Summer Cottage B

CROSS STITCH

ANCHOR		DMC	COLOR
002	•	White	White
109	V	209	Dark Lavender
9046	S	321	Christmas Red
977	H	334	Medium Baby Blue
302	A	743	Medium Yellow
301	Z	744	Pale Yellow
300	M	745	Light Pale Yellow
234	Q	762	Very Light Pearl Gray
128	F	775	Very Light Baby Blue
132	E	797	Royal Blue
256	N	906	Medium Parrot Green
255	7	907	Light Parrot Green
040	C	956	Geranium
050	B	957	Pale Geranium
186	I	959	Medium Sea Green
185	J	964	Light Sea Green
355	P	975	Dark Golden Brown
129	G	3325	Light Baby Blue
899	O	3782	Light Mocha Brown

FRENCH KNOT

ANCHOR		DMC	COLOR
002	•	White	White
132	•	797	Royal Blue

BACKSTITCH

ANCHOR		DMC	COLOR
132	—	797	Royal Blue
256	—	906	Medium Parrot Green
355	—	975	Dark Golden Brown

STRAIGHT STITCH

ANCHOR		DMC	COLOR
132	—	797	Royal Blue
355	—	975	Dark Golden Brown

Gray area indicates last row of previous section of design.

Summer Cottage C

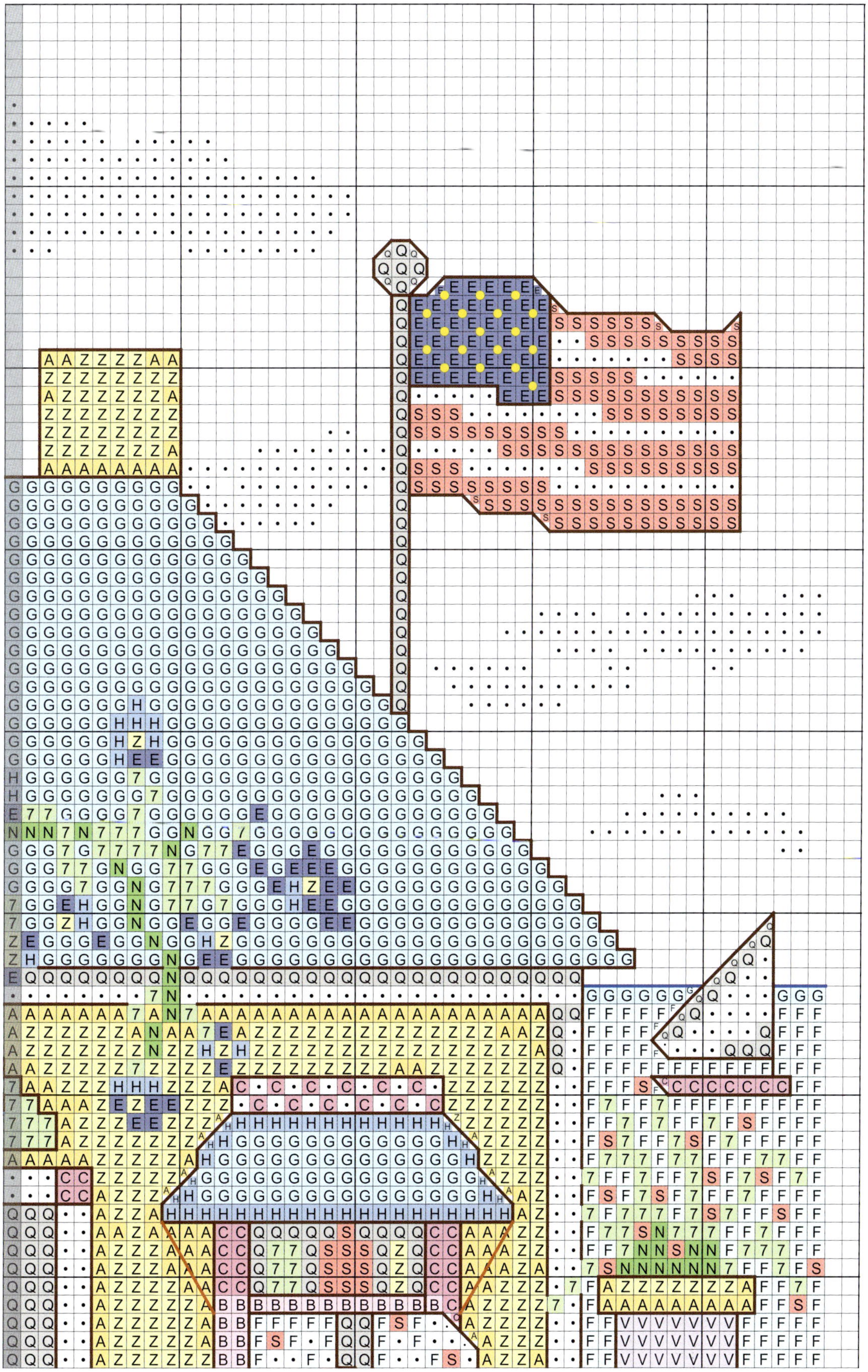

Summer Cottage D

CROSS STITCH

ANCHOR		DMC	COLOR
002	•	White	White
109	V	209	Dark Lavender
9046	S	321	Christmas Red
977	H	334	Medium Baby Blue
302	A	743	Medium Yellow
301	Z	744	Pale Yellow
300	M	745	Light Pale Yellow
234	Q	762	Very Light Pearl Gray
128	F	775	Very Light Baby Blue
132	E	797	Royal Blue
256	N	906	Medium Parrot Green
255	7	907	Light Parrot Green

CROSS STITCH

ANCHOR		DMC	COLOR
040	C	956	Geranium
050	B	957	Pale Geranium
186	I	959	Medium Sea Green
185	J	964	Light Sea Green
355	P	975	Dark Golden Brown
129	G	3325	Light Baby Blue
899	O	3782	Light Mocha Brown

FRENCH KNOT

ANCHOR		DMC	COLOR
002	•	White	White
132	•	797	Royal Blue

BACKSTITCH

ANCHOR	DMC	COLOR
132	797	Royal Blue
256	906	Medium Parrot Green
355	975	Dark Golden Brown

STRAIGHT STITCH

ANCHOR	DMC	COLOR
132	797	Royal Blue
355	975	Dark Golden Brown

Gray area indicates last row of previous section of design.

Summer Cottage E

Project Tip

Keeping Fabric Clean in a Hoop

When using a hoop, try putting a sheet of white tissue paper in the hoop on top of the fabric. Tear away the tissue paper in the area where you are stitching. This keeps oils from your hands from getting on the fabric and helps keep the needlework piece free from stains. And whether you use a hoop or not, always wash and dry your hands completely before starting any stitching.

Autumn Cottage

Enjoy a gorgeous fall day with this charming cottage.

Note: Please read all instructions on page 32 before beginning.

Stitch Count = 123w × 125h

FABRIC SIZE

- One 17" × 17" (43.2cm × 43.2cm) piece of 28-ct. Summer Sky Hand-Dyed Jobelan® by Wichelt Imports (stitched over two threads)

DESIGN SIZE

- 25-ct. = 9 7/8" × 10" (25.1cm × 25.4cm)
- 28-ct. = 8 3/4" × 8 7/8" (22.2cm × 22.5cm)
- 32-ct. = 7 5/8" × 7 3/4" (19.4cm × 19.7cm)

Project Tip

Working with Several Floss Colors

When working with frequent color changes, use several needles to avoid rethreading the same needle over and over. Work a few stitches in one color, bring the needle to the front of the fabric and put it aside. Introduce the next floss color and needle and continue.

AUTUMN COTTAGE CHART DIAGRAM

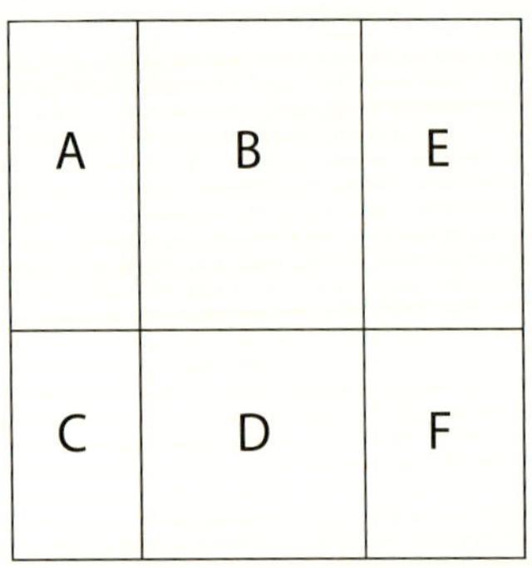

CROSS STITCH

ANCHOR		DMC	COLOR
002	•	White	White
9046	A	321	Christmas Red
398	U	415	Pearl Gray
168	F	597	Turquoise
167	E	598	Light Turquoise
326	N	720	Dark Orange Spice
303	M	742	Light Tangerine
302	L	743	Medium Yellow
301	K	744	Pale Yellow
234	T	762	Very Light Pearl Gray
128	C	775	Very Light Baby Blue
257	I	905	Dark Parrot Green
256	H	906	Medium Parrot Green
255	G	907	Light Parrot Green
1003	O	922	Light Copper
355	R	975	Dark Golden Brown
1001	Q	976	Medium Golden Brown
1002	P	977	Light Golden Brown
292	J	3078	Very Light Golden Yellow
382	S	3371	Black Brown
1037	B	3756	Ultra Very Light Baby Blue
928	D	3811	Very Light Turquoise

BACKSTITCH

ANCHOR		DMC	COLOR
301	—	744	Pale Yellow
355	—	975	Dark Golden Brown
382	—	3371	Black Brown

Gray area indicates last row of previous section of design.

Autumn Cottage A

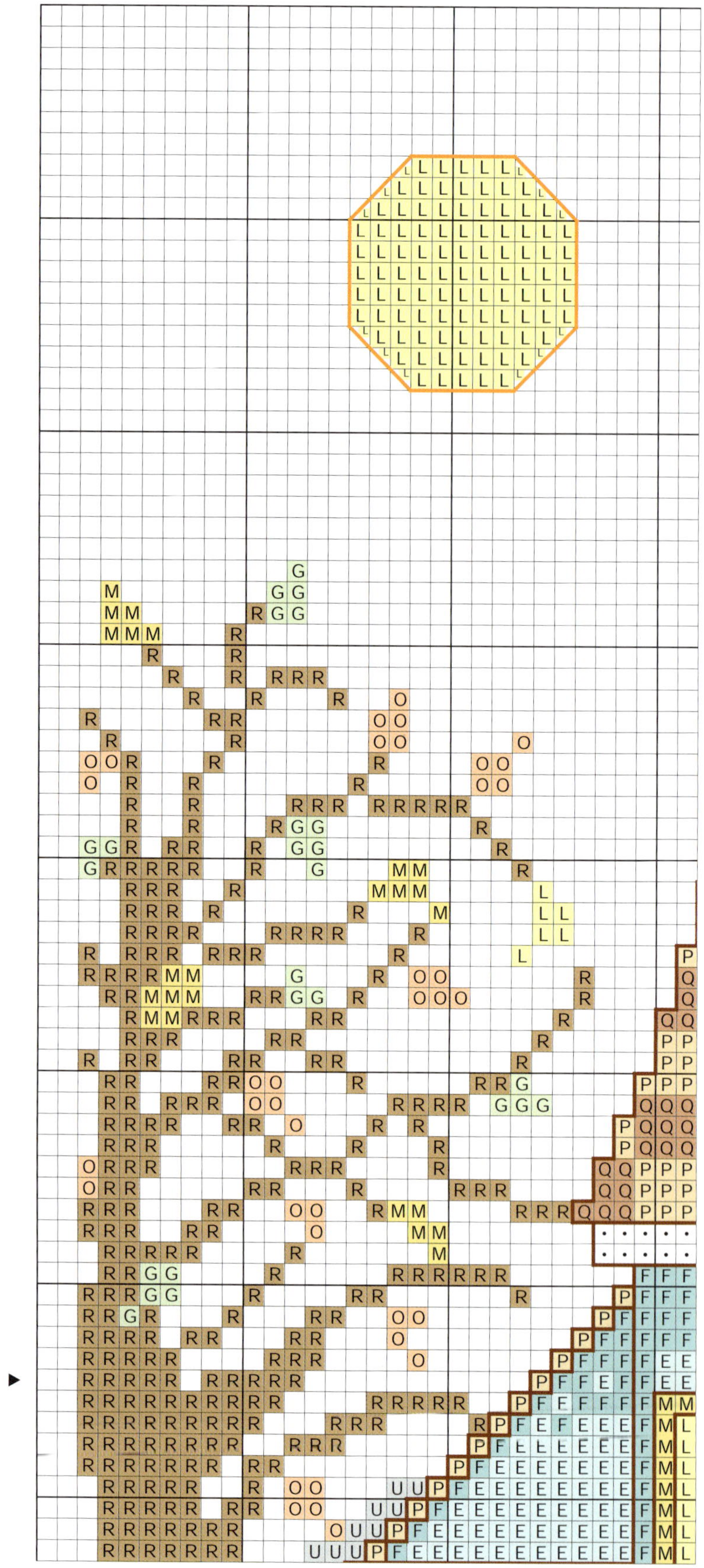

Autumn Cottage B

CROSS STITCH

ANCHOR		DMC	COLOR
002	•	White	White
9046	A	321	Christmas Red
398	U	415	Pearl Gray
168	F	597	Turquoise
167	E	598	Light Turquoise
326	N	720	Dark Orange Spice
303	M	742	Light Tangerine
302	L	743	Medium Yellow
301	K	744	Pale Yellow
234	T	762	Very Light Pearl Gray
128	C	775	Very Light Baby Blue
257	I	905	Dark Parrot Green
256	H	906	Medium Parrot Green
255	G	907	Light Parrot Green
1003	O	922	Light Copper
355	R	975	Dark Golden Brown
1001	Q	976	Medium Golden Brown
1002	P	977	Light Golden Brown
292	J	3078	Very Light Golden Yellow
382	S	3371	Black Brown
1037	B	3756	Ultra Very Light Baby Blue
928	D	3811	Very Light Turquoise

BACKSTITCH

ANCHOR		DMC	COLOR
301	—	744	Pale Yellow
355	—	975	Dark Golden Brown
382	—	3371	Black Brown

Gray area indicates last row of previous section of design.

Autumn Cottage C

Autumn Cottage D

Autumn Cottage E

CROSS STITCH

ANCHOR		DMC	COLOR
002	•	White	White
9046	A	321	Christmas Red
398	U	415	Pearl Gray
168	F	597	Turquoise
167	E	598	Light Turquoise
326	N	720	Dark Orange Spice
303	M	742	Light Tangerine
302	L	743	Medium Yellow
301	K	744	Pale Yellow
234	T	762	Very Light Pearl Gray
128	C	775	Very Light Baby Blue
257	I	905	Dark Parrot Green
256	H	906	Medium Parrot Green
255	G	907	Light Parrot Green
1003	O	922	Light Copper
355	R	975	Dark Golden Brown
1001	Q	976	Medium Golden Brown
1002	P	977	Light Golden Brown
292	J	3078	Very Light Golden Yellow
382	S	3371	Black Brown
1037	B	3756	Ultra Very Light Baby Blue
928	D	3811	Very Light Turquoise

BACKSTITCH

ANCHOR	DMC	COLOR
301	744	Pale Yellow
355	975	Dark Golden Brown
382	3371	Black Brown

Gray area indicates last row of previous section of design.

Autumn Cottage F

Winter Cottage

Get into the holiday spirit
with this festive home.

Note: Please read all instructions on page 32 before beginning.

Stitch Count =125w × 125h

FABRIC SIZE

- One 17" × 17" (43.2cm × 43.2cm) piece of 28-ct. Summer Sky Hand-Dyed Jobelan® by Wichelt Imports (stitched over two threads)

DESIGN SIZE

- 25-ct. = 10" × 10" (25.4cm × 25.4cm)
- 28-ct. = 8 7/8" × 8 7/8" (22.5cm × 22.5cm)
- 32-ct. = 7 7/8" × 7 7/8" (20.0cm × 20.0cm)

Project Tip

Storing Seasonal Needlework

To ensure that seasonal needlework items stay looking their best from year to year, it is important to store them properly. Washable items should be cleaned with a mild soap and water solution to remove any stains or dirt. Allow pieces to dry completely so no moisture remains. Wrap all items in acid-free tissue paper and place in an acid-free box for storage. (Plastic bags or bins can trap moisture and cause mildew and staining.) The box should then be stored in a dark place, free from humidity or extreme temperatures; an interior closet is best. Linens should be refolded twice a year to prevent any fabric creases from becoming permanent.

WINTER COTTAGE CHART DIAGRAM

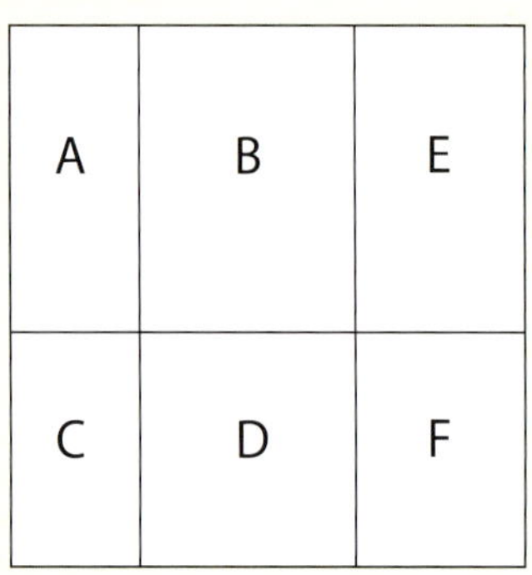

CROSS STITCH

ANCHOR		DMC	COLOR
002	•	White	White
1006	M	304	Medium Christmas Red
9046	L	321	Christmas Red
046	K	666	Bright Christmas Red
302	P	743	Medium Yellow
301	C	744	Pale Yellow
234	Y	762	Very Light Pearl Gray
132	R	797	Royal Blue
257	G	905	Dark Parrot Green
256	H	906	Medium Parrot Green
255	J	907	Light Parrot Green
355	A	975	Dark Golden Brown
1001	B	976	Medium Golden Brown
1040	W	3023	Light Brown Gray
382	F	3371	Black Brown
1032	S	3752	Very Light Antique Blue
1031	V	3753	Ultra Very Light Antique Blue
1037	D	3756	Ultra Very Light Baby Blue
295	Q	3822	Light Straw

FRENCH KNOT

ANCHOR		DMC	COLOR
002	•	White	White
046	•	666	Bright Christmas Red

BACKSTITCH

ANCHOR		DMC	COLOR
355	—	975	Dark Golden Brown
382	—	3371	Black Brown

Gray area indicates last row of previous section of design.

Winter Cottage A

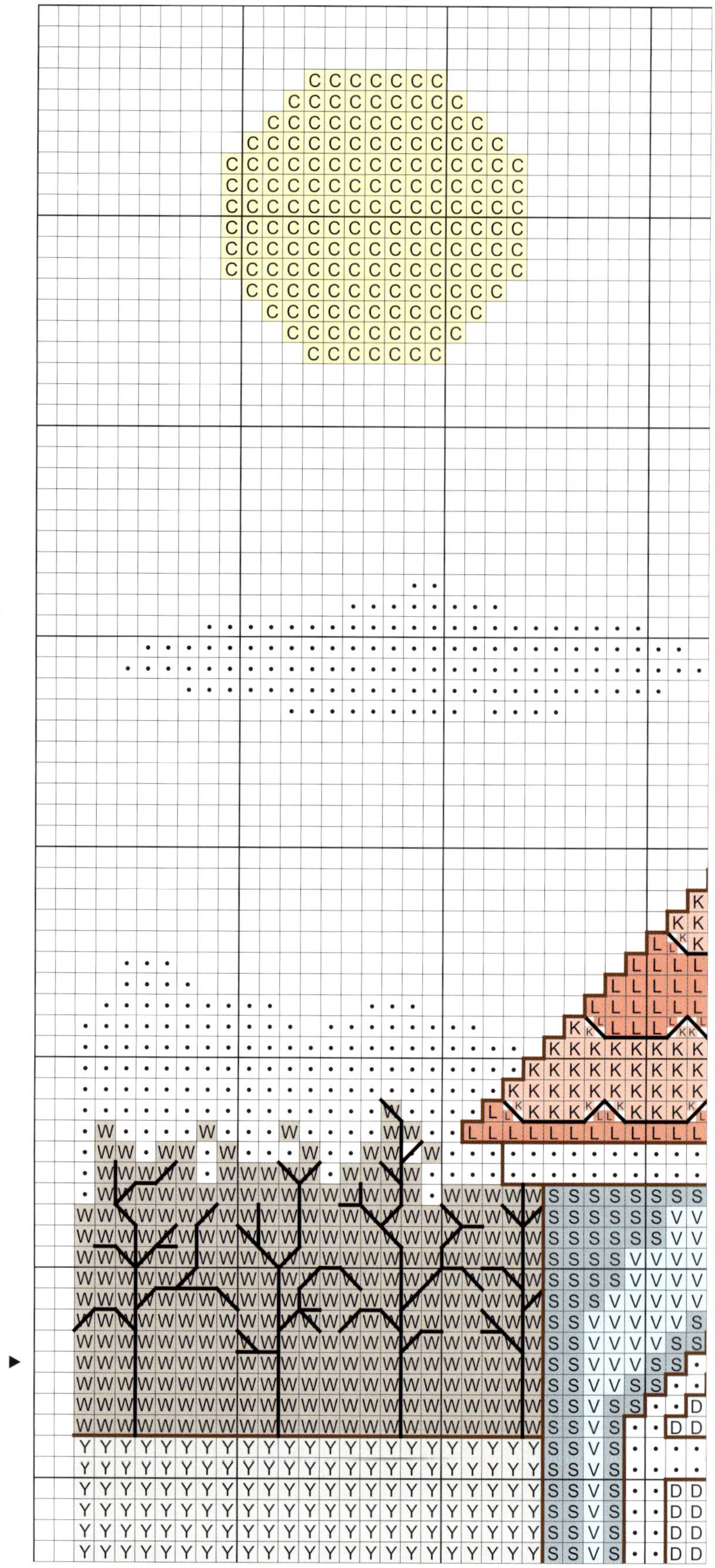

Winter Cottage B

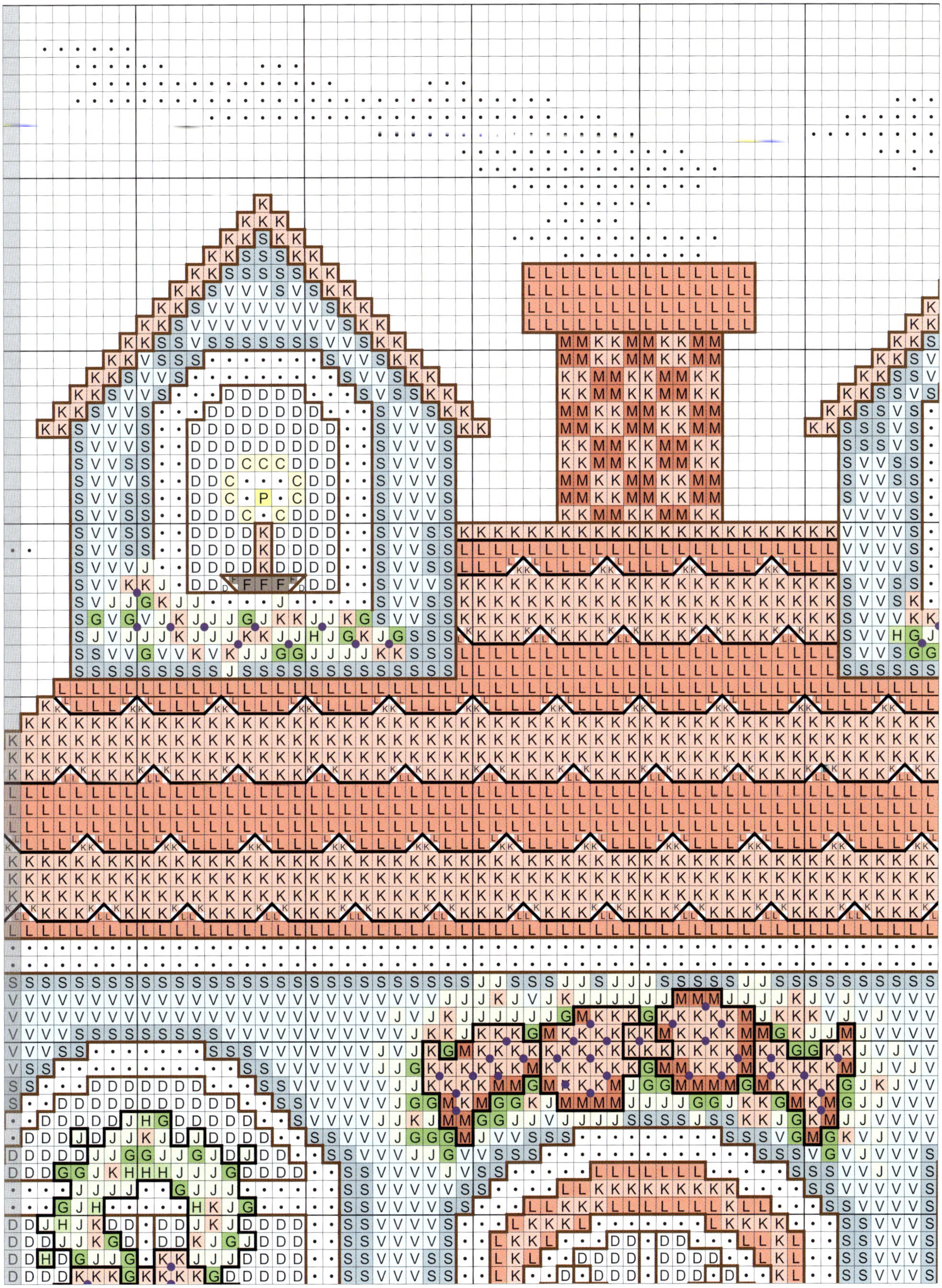

Winter Cottage C

CROSS STITCH

ANCHOR		DMC	COLOR
002	•	White	White
1006	M	304	Medium Christmas Red
9046	L	321	Christmas Red
046	K	666	Bright Christmas Red
302	P	743	Medium Yellow
301	C	744	Pale Yellow
234	Y	762	Very Light Pearl Gray
132	R	797	Royal Blue
257	G	905	Dark Parrot Green
256	H	906	Medium Parrot Green
255	J	907	Light Parrot Green
355	A	975	Dark Golden Brown
1001	B	976	Medium Golden Brown
1040	W	3023	Light Brown Gray
382	F	3371	Black Brown
1032	S	3752	Very Light Antique Blue
1031	V	3753	Ultra Very Light Antique Blue
1037	D	3756	Ultra Very Light Baby Blue
295	Q	3822	Light Straw

FRENCH KNOT

ANCHOR		DMC	COLOR
002	•	White	White
046	•	666	Bright Christmas Red

BACKSTITCH

ANCHOR		DMC	COLOR
355	—	975	Dark Golden Brown
382	—	3371	Black Brown

Gray area indicates last row of previous section of design.

Winter Cottage D

Winter Cottage E

CROSS STITCH

ANCHOR		DMC	COLOR
002	•	White	White
1006	M	304	Medium Christmas Red
9046	L	321	Christmas Red
046	K	666	Bright Christmas Red
302	P	743	Medium Yellow
301	C	744	Pale Yellow
234	Y	762	Very Light Pearl Gray
132	R	797	Royal Blue
257	G	905	Dark Parrot Green
256	H	906	Medium Parrot Green
255	J	907	Light Parrot Green
355	A	975	Dark Golden Brown
1001	B	976	Medium Golden Brown
1040	W	3023	Light Brown Gray
382	F	3371	Black Brown
1032	S	3752	Very Light Antique Blue
1031	V	3753	Ultra Very Light Antique Blue
1037	D	3756	Ultra Very Light Baby Blue
295	Q	3822	Light Straw

FRENCH KNOT

ANCHOR		DMC	COLOR
002	•	White	White
046	•	666	Bright Christmas Red

BACKSTITCH

ANCHOR		DMC	COLOR
355	—	975	Dark Golden Brown
382	—	3371	Black Brown

Gray area indicates last row of previous section of design.

Winter Cottage F

General Instructions

Getting Started

For most projects, the starting point is at the center. Every chart has arrows that indicate the horizontal and vertical centers. With your finger, trace along the grid to the point where the two centers meet. Compare a symbol at the center of the chart to the key and choose which floss color to stitch first. To find the center of the fabric, fold it into quarters and finger-crease.

Cut the floss into 15" lengths and separate all six strands. Recombine the appropriate number of strands and thread them into a blunt-tip needle. Use two strands of floss to work cross stitches and quarter cross stitches. Use one strand of floss to work backstitches, straight stitches, and French knots.

To Secure Thread at the Beginning

The most common way to secure the beginning tail of the thread is to hold it on the wrong side of the fabric under the first four or five stitches.

To Secure Thread at the End

To finish, slip the threaded needle under previously stitched threads on the wrong side of the fabric for four or five stitches, weaving the thread back and forth a few times. Clip the thread.

Framing Your Pieces

Iron the finished needlework on the wrong side using a dry pressing cloth and medium temperature setting; do not steam. Accurately measure the length and width of your completed piece before purchasing a mat or frame. Consulting a professional framer or art supply store to mat and frame your design is recommended.

Cross Stitch

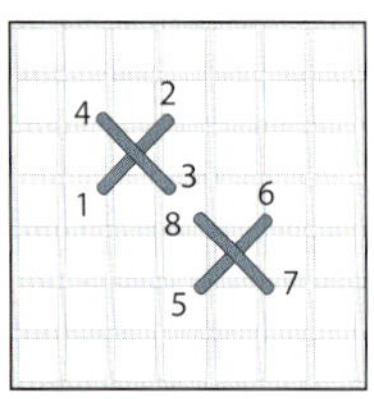

Make one cross stitch for each symbol on the chart. For horizontal rows, stitch the first diagonal of each stitch in the row. Work back across the row, completing each stitch. On linen and evenweave fabrics, work the stitches over two threads as shown in the diagram. For aida cloth, each stitch fills one square. You also can work cross stitches in the reverse direction. Remember to embroider the stitches uniformly—that is, always work the top half of each stitch in the same direction.

Quarter Cross Stitch

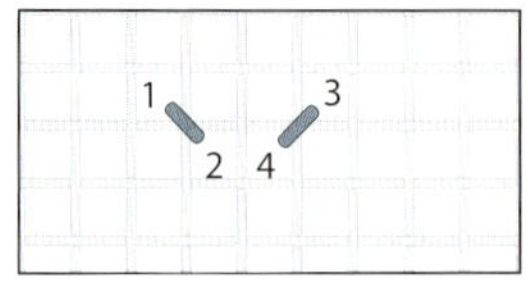

To obtain rounded shapes in a design, use quarter cross stitches. On linen and evenweave fabrics, a quarter stitch will extend from the corner to the center intersection of the threads. To make quarter cross stitches on aida cloth, estimate the center of the square. This stitch may slant in any direction.

Backstitch

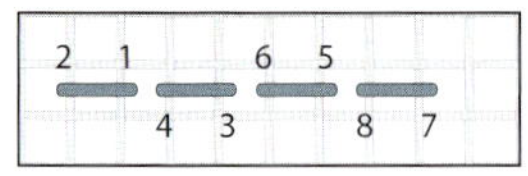

Working from right to left, bring the needle up from the back side of the fabric, one stitch length from your starting point. Begin the next stitch by inserting the needle at your starting point and back up two stitch lengths away. Continue, keeping all the stitches the same length.

French Knot

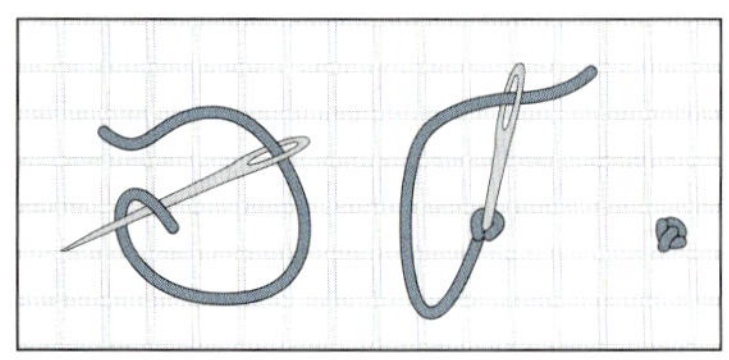

Bring the threaded needle through the fabric and wrap the floss around the needle as shown. Tighten the twists and return the needle through the fabric in the same place. The floss will slide through the wrapped thread to make the knot.

Straight Stitch

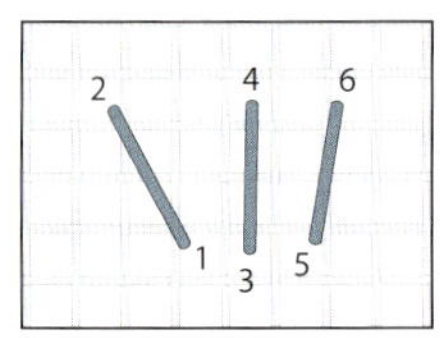

Bring the needle up from the back side of the fabric, then bring the needle down through the fabric in the desired spot to make a stitch of the desired length.

Produced by Herrschners, Inc., for distribution exclusively by Leisure Arts, Inc., 104 Champs Blvd., STE 100, Maumelle, AR 72113-6738, leisurearts.com.